Coronavirus A-Z

*How to Understand Vocabulary Words
connected to the Coronavirus*

**Author Lyric Williams
Co-Author Janice Wilson
Illustrated By: Laila Malik Bey**

Copyright ©2020 by Lyric Williams and Janice Wilson

All rights reserved.

No part of this book may be reproduced or transmitted in any form or by any means, electronic or mechanical, including photocopying, recording, or by any information storage and retrieval system, without permission in writing from the copyright author, except for the use of brief quotations in a book review.

ISBN: 978-1-970135-77-0 paperback

Published in the United States by Pen2Pad Ink Publishing.

Lyric Williams and Janice Wilson retains the right to all images.

This book is dedicated to my family and all the children all over the world. My name is Lyric Symone Williams. I am currently 8 years old and in the third grade. This is my first attempt at writing with the assistance of my grandma, Janice. I hope that *Coronavirus A-Z* will give you a better understanding of the pandemic that was discovered in Wuhan, China on December 31, 2019.

This alphabetical book of words will give the reader a better understanding of words connected to the Coronavirus known as COVID-19.

Awareness of COVID-19 was first reported December 31, 2019, in Wuhan, China.

B

Blood plasma can be taken from a recovered COVID-19 patient and transfused into a person suffering from the Coronavirus.

C

Coronaviruses are a large family of viruses. Most of the viruses in this family are harmless for humans.

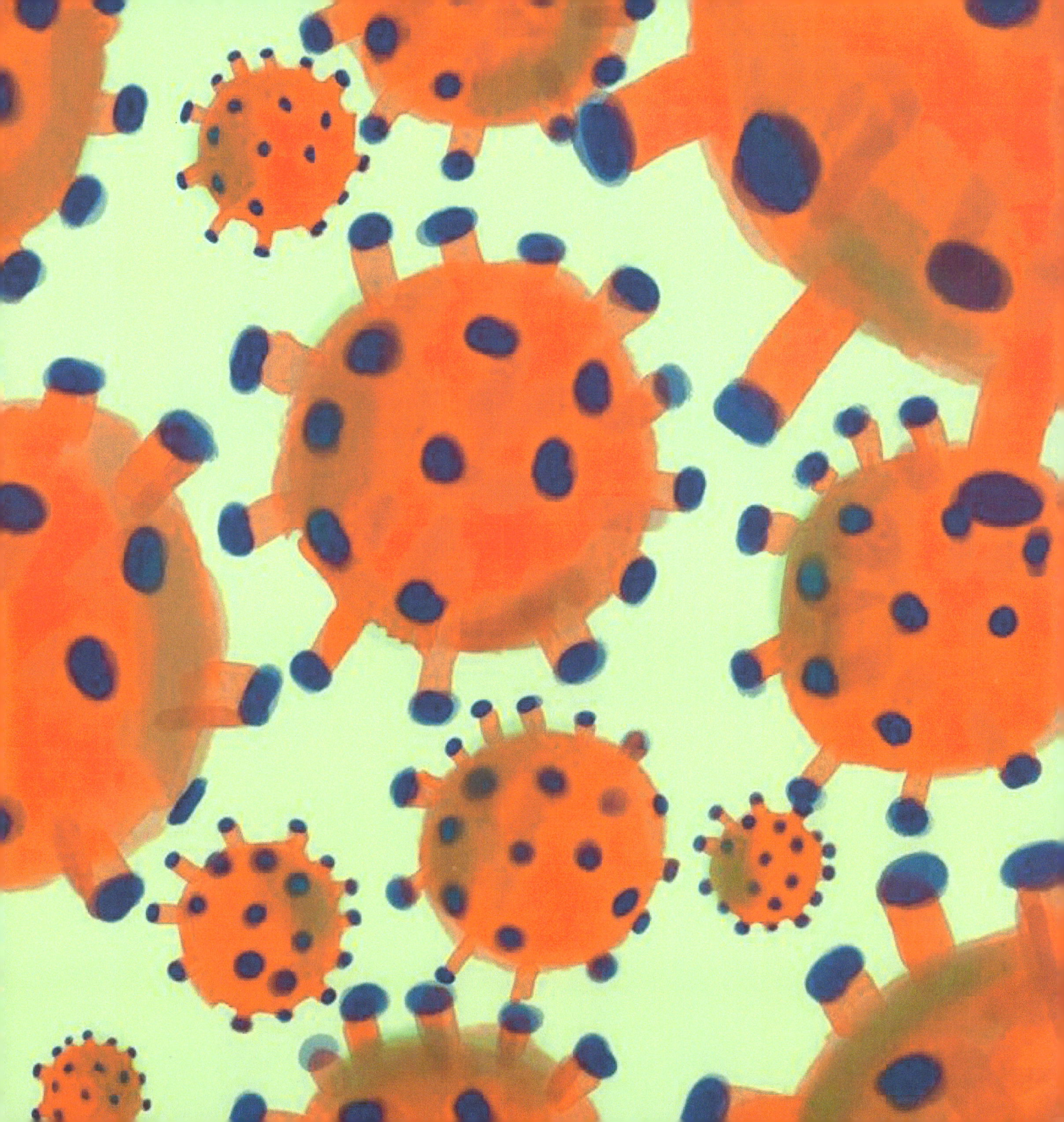

D

Doctors Without Borders is a team of doctors who worked on projects around the world to fight the spread of coronavirus.

E

Exhaling small droplets of saliva
from the mouth can infect a person.

F

Fatalities or deaths from the Coronavirus disease increased daily, due to the need of a vaccine, lack of delayed lockdowns, and a lack of social distancing.

G

Germs are microorganisms that cause disease. Germs can be removed through disinfecting all surfaces with bleach or Lysol.

H

Hand hygiene is very important!
Wash your hands often with soap and
water and for at least 20 seconds.

I

Infection control measures like good handwashing, wearing a mask, coughing into your elbow, and sneeze etiquette are effective and important for COVID-19 prevention.

J

Johns Hopkins University, a private medical research university in Baltimore, Maryland, is working on a vaccine.

K

Kidneys are bean shaped organs that help pass urine, but they will shut down when the blood does not supply enough oxygen to the body.

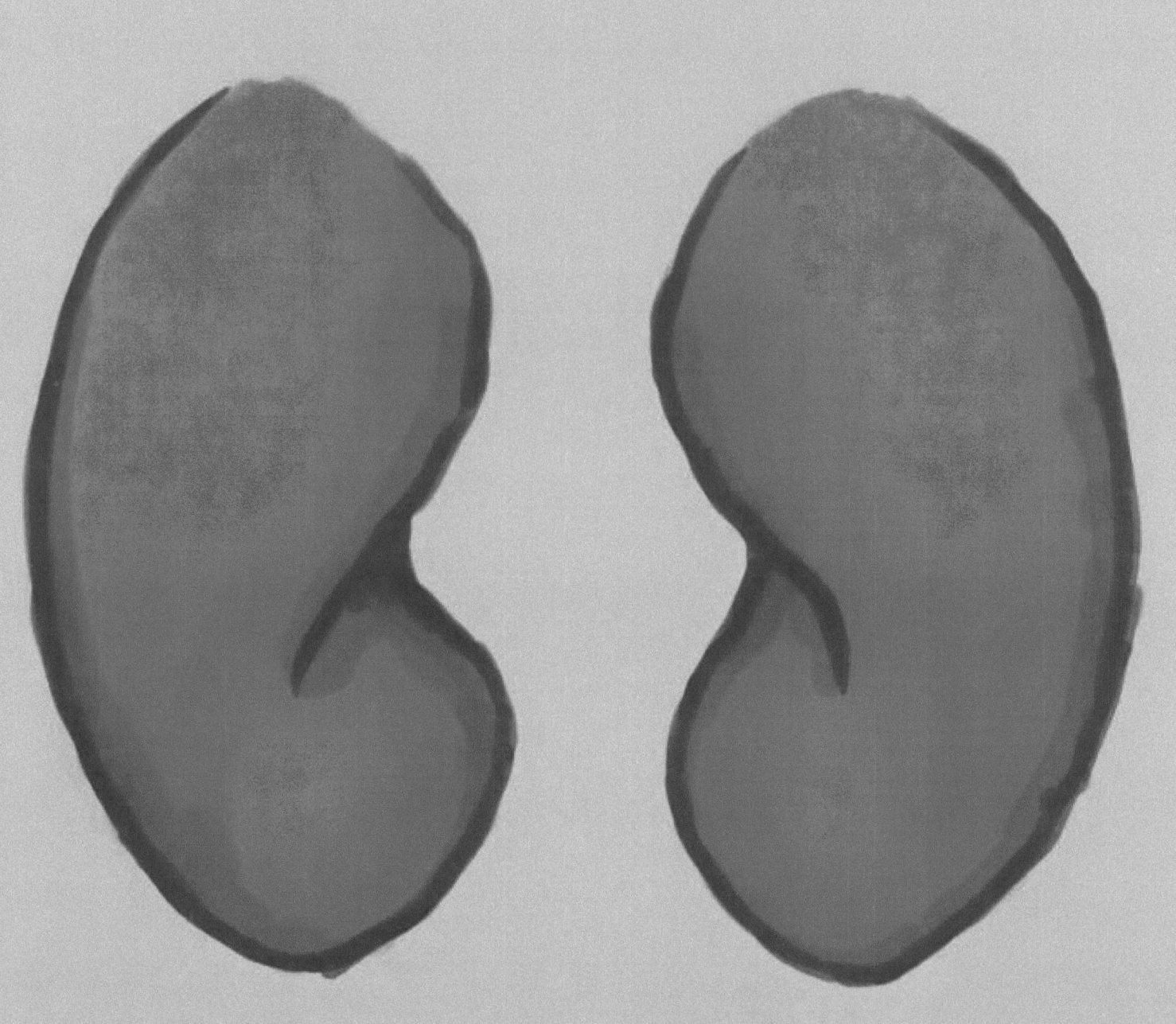

L

Lungs are a pair of air-filled organs for breathing and will shut down when not supplied with enough oxygen.

M

Masks are worn over the mouth and nose to stop the spread of saliva and mucus droplets.

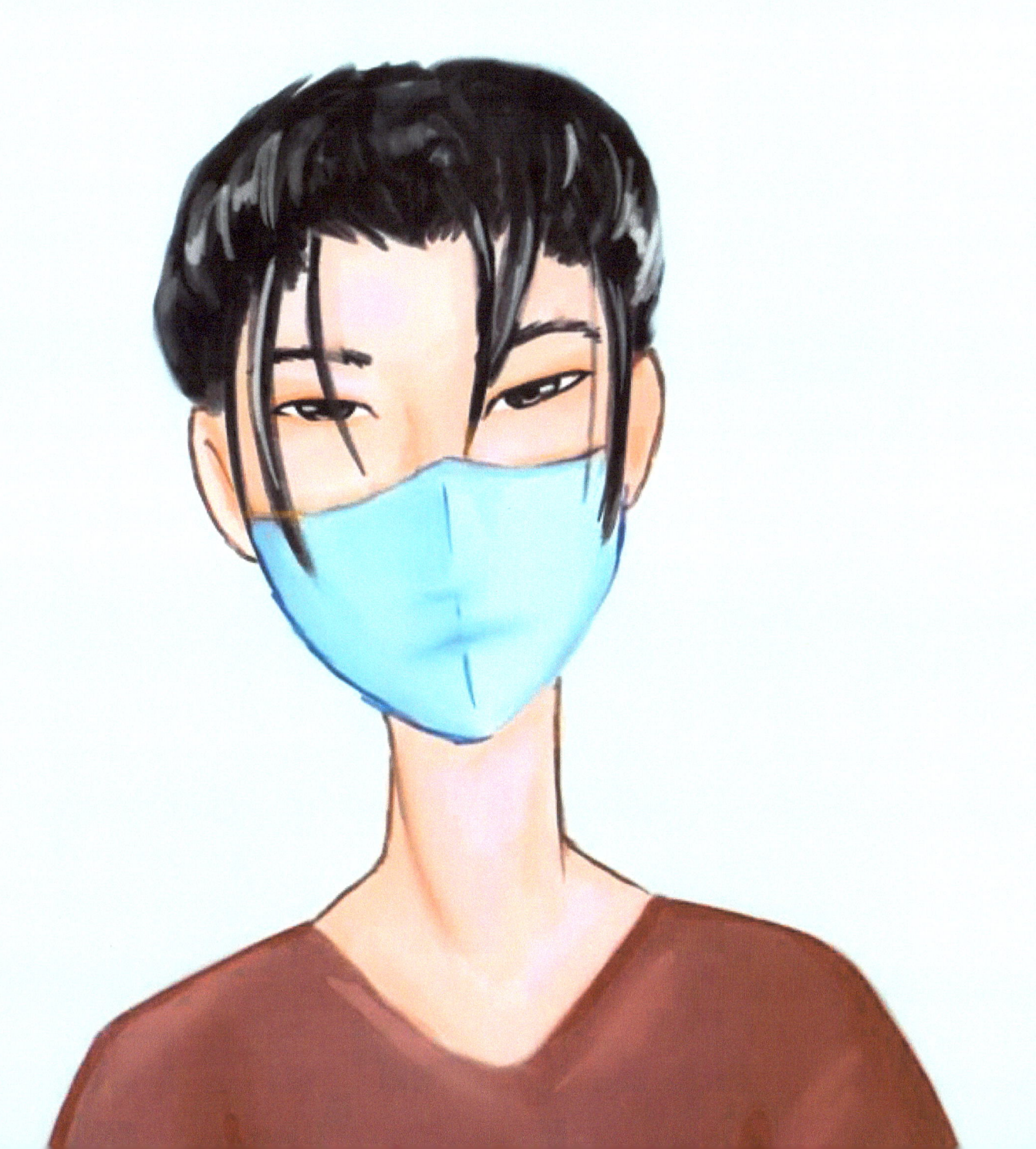

N

Negative nasal secretions mean that a person does not have COVID-19.

O

Organizations like the CDC and the World Health Organization with leaders like Dr. Anthony Fauci help give important information about the disease.

P

Pandemic is the outbreak of a disease
over a whole country or the world.

Q

Quarantine is going into isolation when you become infected with a disease such as COVID-19.

R

The respiratory system includes lungs that help you inhale air and exhale carbon dioxide.

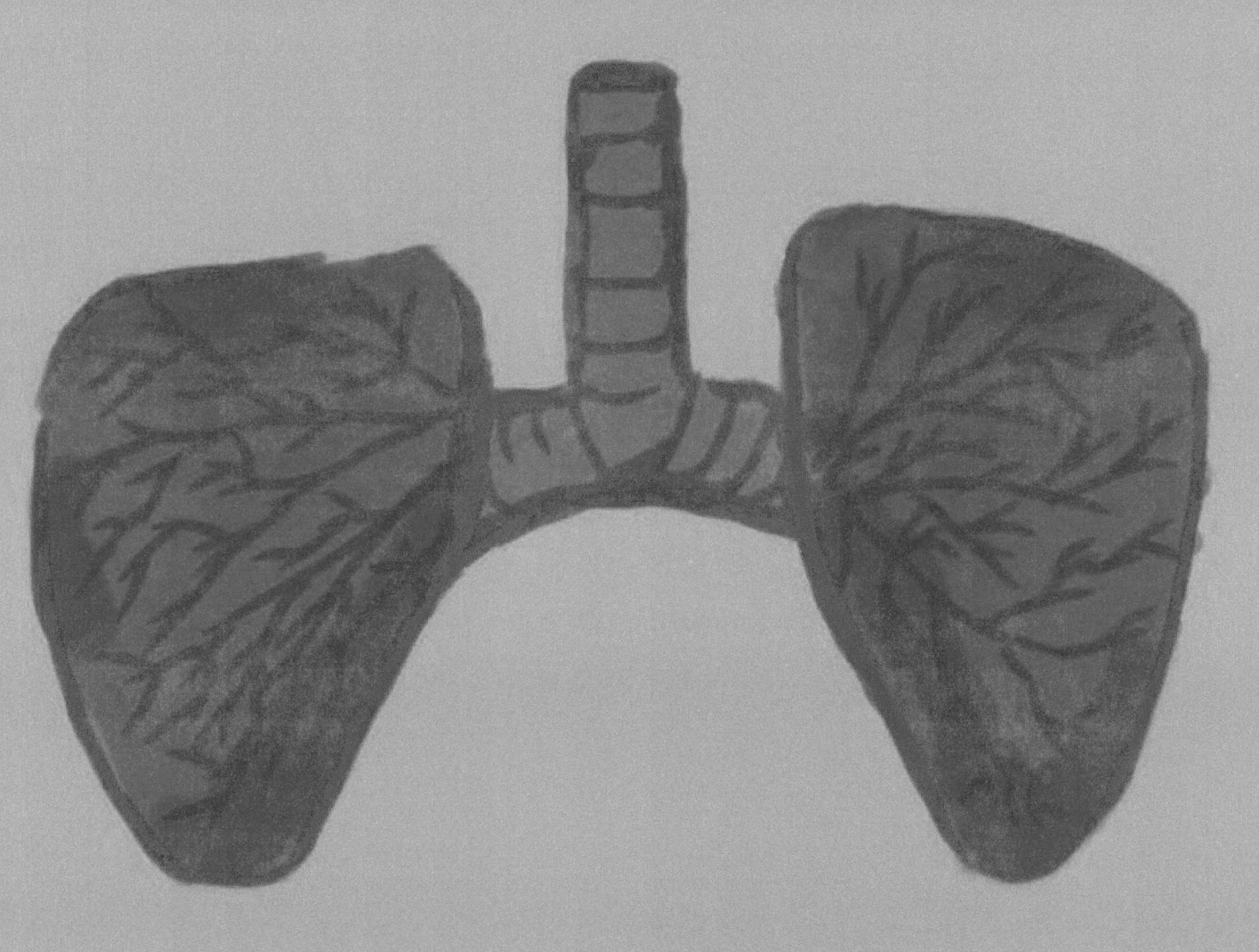

S

Spreading the Coronavirus can be prevented by wearing your mask, washing your hands for 20 seconds, standing 6 feet apart, and staying at home.

T

Temperatures above 100°F are a sign of infection.

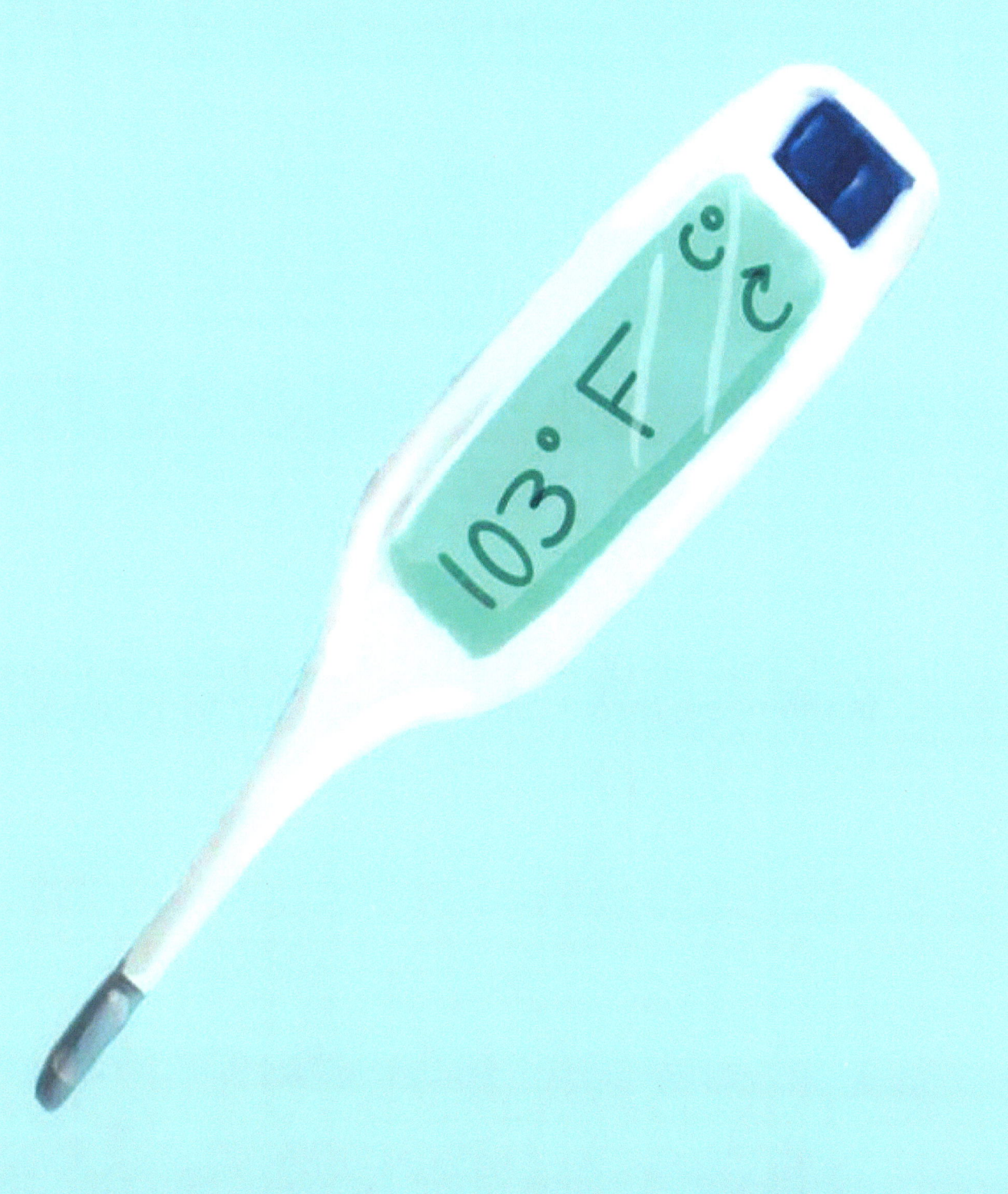

U

An upper respiratory infection is a viral infection that affects the nose, throat, and airways for 7 to 10 days.

V

Vaccine medicines, such as Remdesivir,
are used to treat COVID-19.

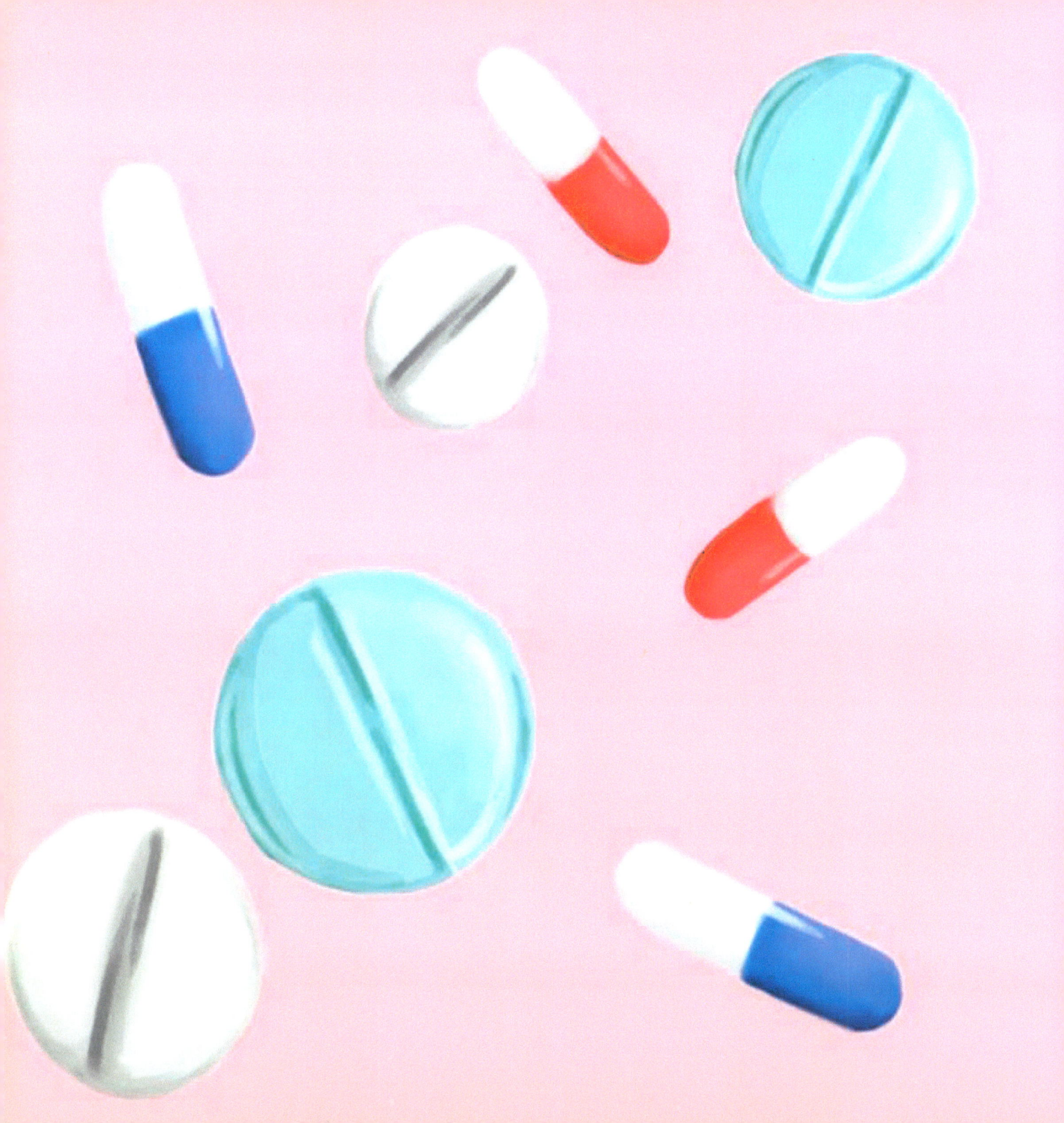

Wuhan is the capital of Central China's Hubei province that is divided by the Yangtze and Hans rivers.

CHINA

Hubei Province

Wuhan

X-Ray is a type of radiation electromagnetic wave that takes a picture of the inside of the body.

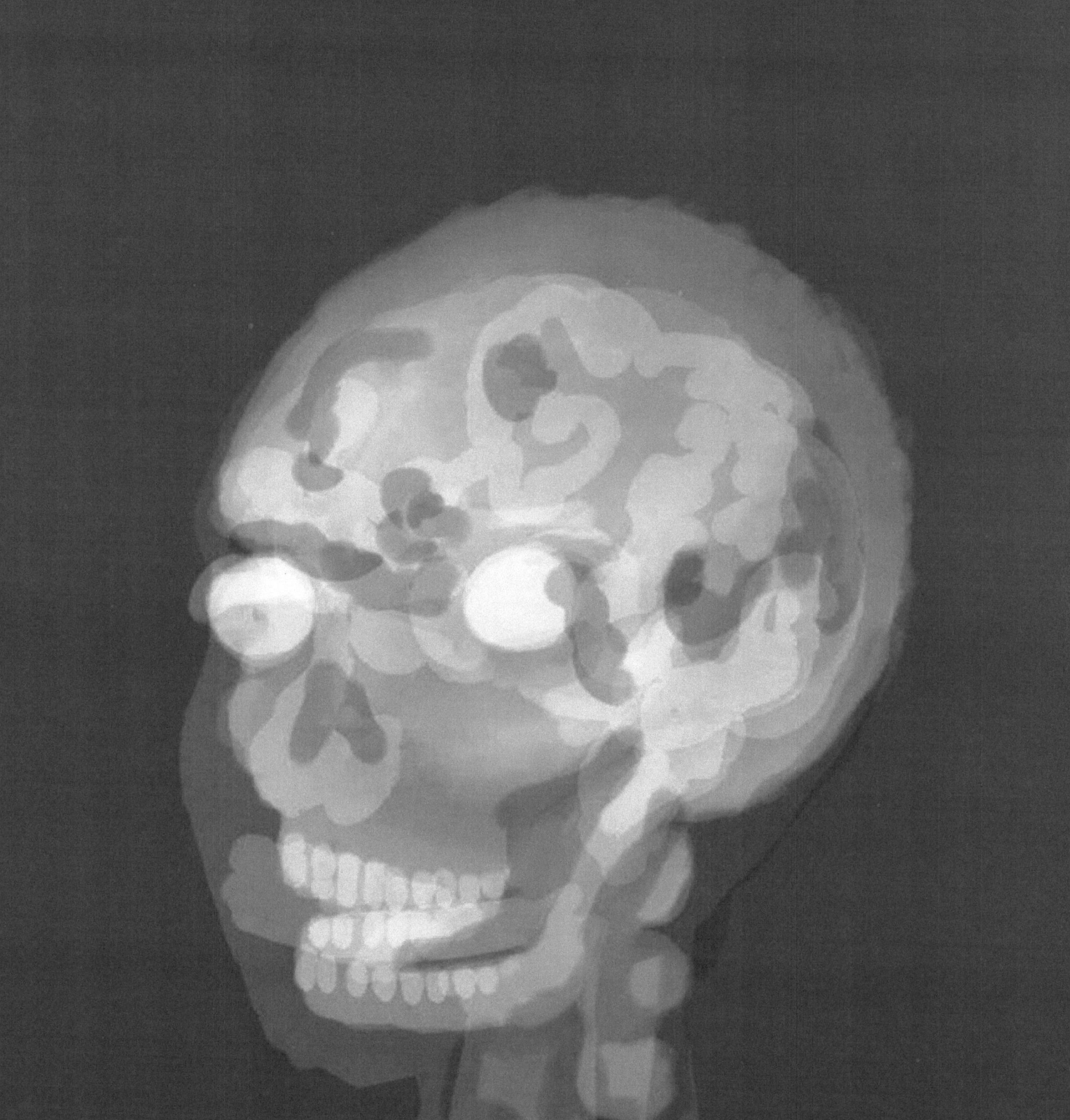

Y

Young kids and adults can die from the Coronavirus.

RIP
JOHNATHAN DOE
1976-2020

RIP
JANE DOE
2016-2020

Z

Zoo animals, like the lion and tiger, also showed symptoms of respiratory problems.

Other Books by
Lyric Williams and Janice Wilson

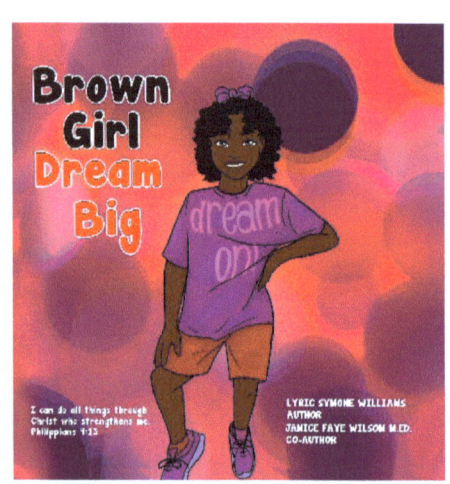
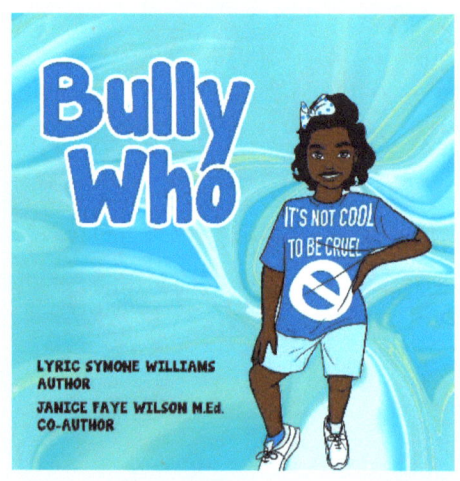

www.ingramcontent.com/pod-product-compliance
Lightning Source LLC
LaVergne TN
LVHW070450080526
838202LV00035B/2795